THE
STRATEGIES
CONFIDENCE
FOR
PLAYBOOK

LIFELONG SUCCESS

THE
STRATEGIES
CONFIDENCE
FOR
PLAYBOOK
LIFELONG SUCCESS

A WORKBOOK JOURNAL BY
SYLVIA CRAWLEY SPANN

The Confidence Playbook: Strategies for Lifelong Success
Sylvia Crawley Spann

All rights reserved
First Edition, 2024
© Sylvia Crawley Spann, 2024

No part of this publication may be reproduced, or stored in
a retrieval system, or transmitted in any form by means of
electronic, mechanical, photocopying or otherwise, without prior
written permission from the author.

TABLE OF CONTENTS

INTRODUCTION 1

CHAPTER 1
PLAY TO YOUR STRENGTHS 3
    Understanding the Strategy:..3
    Recognizing Your Strengths:..4
    Maximizing Your Strengths:...5
    Why Comparison Destroys Confidence:.............................6
    Reflecting on My Journey: 6

CHAPTER 2
PRACTICE MAKES PERMANENT 11
    Understanding the Strategy:... 11
    Consistency is Key:... 12
    Repetition Breeds Mastery:.. 13

CHAPTER 3
LEARN FROM EVERY LOSS 21
    Understanding the Strategy:.. 21
    Resilience: The Key to Learning from Losses................... 22
    Why Failure Is an Essential Part of Success:.................... 23
    How to Learn from Failure:... 23
    Turning Setbacks into Confidence:.................................... 24

CHAPTER 4
CONTROL YOUR INNER DIALOGUE 31
    Understanding the Strategy:.. 31
    The Power of Positive Self-Talk:....................................... 32

Reflecting on My Journey: 33
How to Control Your Inner Dialogue: 34

CHAPTER 5
VISUALIZE YOUR SUCCESS 38
Understanding the Strategy: 38
Reflecting on My Journey: 39
How to Visualize Your Success: 42

CHAPTER 6
SURROUND YOURSELF WITH CHAMPIONS 46
Understanding the Strategy: 46
Bounce Pass to Me: 47
Building Your Network of Champions: 49
The Power of Accountability: 50
Becoming a Champion for Others: 51

CHAPTER 7
CELEBRATE YOUR WINS 55
Understanding the Strategy: 55
Reflecting on My Journey: 56
Why Celebrating Your Wins Matters: 58
Celebrating the Small Wins: 59
Here's how you can start celebrating the small wins in your life: 59

CONCLUSION
THE JOURNEY TO LIFELONG CONFIDENCE 64
The Power of Daily Action: 65
Embracing Setbacks as Part of the Journey: 65
The Importance of Self-Reflection: 66
Living with Confidence Every Day: 66
Putting Your Playbook into Action: 67
Final Thoughts: 68

ABOUT THE AUTHOR 69
ACKNOWLEDGEMENT 71

INTRODUCTION

Welcome to The Confidence Playbook, a unique workbook, and journal designed to help you build unshakable confidence and achieve success in all areas of life. Whether preparing for a major life decision, chasing a big goal, or simply trying to improve your daily mindset, this book will be your guide.

I'm Sylvia Crawley Spann, and my journey as an athlete, coach, and mentor has been filled with challenges, triumphs, and countless lessons about confidence. From winning a National Championship in college basketball to making history as the first woman to perform a blindfolded dunk in the ABL slam dunk contest, confidence wasn't just something I was born with—it's something I learned, practiced, and perfected.

This workbook will walk you through seven powerful strategies that helped me win on and off the court. But this isn't just about my story—it's about yours. Each chapter includes reflections, exercises, and journaling prompts to help you develop your Confidence Playbook. These strategies and plays you read in this book will only work if you run them. So, I challenge you to play to win by taking time after each chapter to answer the questions so that you can develop, practice, and maintain the confidence you need to gain a higher level of success than you are currently experiencing.

Let's get started.

CHAPTER 1
PLAY TO YOUR STRENGTHS

UNDERSTANDING THE STRATEGY:

Confidence doesn't come from trying to be someone you're not—it comes from embracing and owning who you are. In life, just like in sports, success comes from recognizing and relying on your unique strengths. Too often, we waste time focusing on our weaknesses or comparing ourselves to others, thinking that what we don't have is what matters most. But the truth is, your strengths are your foundation for success, and knowing them is the key to unlocking your confidence.

Each individual possesses a unique combination of abilities, talents, and gifts that distinguish them from others. When you are aware of your own value, you approach challenges with greater confidence, knowing you have the tools needed to succeed. It's not about claiming to have all the answers or striving for perfection—it's about effectively utilizing your existing skills to overcome obstacles and capitalize on opportunities. Whether your strengths lie in problem-solving, communication, leadership, or creative thinking, these qualities form the foundation of your confidence.

The trap many of us fall into is comparison. We look at someone else's achievements or talents and assume we need to be like them to succeed. But the truth is, that comparison is the enemy of confidence. Every individual is on their journey, and what works for someone else may not work for you. Confidence begins when you stop comparing yourself to others and start recognizing that your strengths, while different, are just as valuable. When you own your strengths, you stop doubting yourself. You realize that no one else can play the game the way you can, and that's where your power lies.

So, how do you play to your strengths? It starts with self-awareness. You have to take the time to identify what you're good at—what comes naturally to you. But it doesn't stop there. Once you know your strengths, you have to amplify them. Use them as a driving force in everything you do. Let them shape the way you approach challenges, the way you set goals, and the way you tackle opportunities. By leaning into your strengths, you'll not only build confidence, but you'll also achieve success on your terms.

RECOGNIZING YOUR STRENGTHS:
Recognizing your strengths is an essential step in the journey to building confidence. Often, we don't give enough thought to the things we're naturally good at because we take them for granted. But these are the very traits that can set you apart. Strengths are not limited to skills acquired through training or education—they can also include personal qualities such as resilience, adaptability, creativity, empathy, or even humor. Any attribute that enhances the way you navigate life is a strength worth recognizing and celebrating.

Take a moment to reflect on situations where you've felt most at ease, where challenges seemed easier to overcome, or where you've received praise from others. What were you doing in those moments? What traits were you using? Sometimes, our greatest strengths are hidden in the things we don't think twice about because they come so naturally.

MAXIMIZING YOUR STRENGTHS:

Once you've identified your strengths, it's time to maximize them. Here's how you can do that:

1. Refine and Develop Them:
- Just because you're naturally good at something doesn't mean there's no room for improvement. Spend time refining your strengths. For instance, if you're great at communication, try to become a more effective speaker or writer. If creativity is your strength, continue to explore new ways to challenge your imagination.

2. Apply Your Strengths to New Challenges:
- Don't keep your strengths confined to one area of your life. If you're a good leader at work, think about how those leadership skills can be applied in other contexts, like in your community or personal life. If you excel in creative problem-solving, use that skill in different areas where it may not seem immediately applicable.

3. Lean on Your Strengths in Times of Doubt:
- When you face uncertainty or difficult moments, remind yourself of your strengths. Trust that you have the tools to navigate any challenge because you've done it before. Use past successes as evidence of your capabilities, and let your strengths guide your decisions.

4. Celebrate Your Strengths:
- Recognize and celebrate the unique abilities you have. Give yourself credit for what you do well. Don't wait for someone else to validate your talents—acknowledge them yourself. When you celebrate your strengths, you build the foundation for self-confidence.

WHY COMPARISON DESTROYS CONFIDENCE:

It's natural to compare yourself to others—we all do it from time to time. But comparison can be a dangerous habit when it comes to building confidence. When you measure yourself against others, you're often only seeing the highlight reel of their lives and achievements, not the struggles and imperfections behind the scenes. This creates an unrealistic benchmark that makes you feel inadequate.

To avoid falling into the comparison trap, it's essential to shift your focus back to your own journey. The goal isn't to mirror someone else, but to become the best version of yourself. Your strengths, experiences, and path are uniquely yours, and that is something to take pride in. When you stop trying to conform to someone else's standards and start embracing what sets you apart, you'll discover a deeper sense of confidence.

* * *

Bounce pass to me:

REFLECTING ON MY JOURNEY:

In high school and college, I played the Center position. The Center is usually the tallest and/or strongest player on the team that stands closest to the basket. The Center is usually not the one shooting 3pt and mid-range shots, their job is shooting high-percentage lay-ups right at the basket and on defense to prevent others from scoring easy lay-ups near the basket. Well, as a Center, I was usually the thinnest and on paper, the physically weakest player on my team. I knew this because in the weight room when we had to test to see what our maximum weights were for bench presses, leg presses, and pull-ups I always lifted the least amount of weight. My coaches always preached that our team was only strong as our weakest player and challenged me to get stronger so the team could be stronger. They met with my

Strength and Conditioning Coach and told them that they wanted him to put 25 extra pounds on me so that I could get stronger. It was very clear that I had a long way to go to be the type of Center that my team wanted and needed. I started to internalize how I was being treated, and my confidence level took a big hit. Although I never gained the 25 pounds that they required of me, the whole situation made me mentally tougher, and I learned to play stronger than what I physically was during my college career. In all, I had a pretty good college career and ended it as a National Champion.

However, I got a chance to train with the Chicago Bulls Strength and Conditioner Coach, Al Vermeil. Upon arrival, he took me through a series of tests for vertical jumping and lateral movement. They measured my wingspan and worked on my core strength. They were very excited about my athleticism and informed me that I had tested higher than any other woman that Nike had ever tested in their facility. As you can imagine, it was refreshing to hear Coaches excited about my physique for once. They informed me that by jumping off two feet I tested very average, but with a step or a running start, it was off the charts. They asked me how many points and rebounds I averaged in college as a Center. When I told them that I averaged around 10 points and 5 rebounds, he was not surprised. He explained that playing as a Center around the basket put me at a disadvantage because stronger post players could be physical with me and even players shorter than me could win position for rebounds. But if I was to take a step or two away from the basket there was no female player that could stop me from getting a rebound or scoring a point. They said that all I had to do was use my god-gifted ability to jump higher and run faster than opponents.

And I took that to heart! It was music to my ears, and actually what I always thought but knew wasn't my role as one of the tallest members on my team. However, the Pros were different, on this level

I was always the tallest. So on the Pro player, I focused more on my strengths. Although I was still thin and not physically strong, I knew I could jump higher than most post players, and run faster, and I had a very high basketball IQ. So, I transitioned to the Forward position and started to play outside in the short corner or high post area. From those positions I could drive past my man to the basket versus standing on the block and letting someone push me off my position. I was now making my opponents play my game instead of me playing into their hands. Meanwhile, my body started to mature, and I started to turn body mass to muscle. I had a much better Pro career and played with much more confidence because I focused on my strengths while still working on my weaknesses.

* * *

Chest pass to you:
Your Turn:

- Identify Your Strengths:
  Take some time to reflect on what you're naturally good at. List 5 strengths you possess, whether in your personal or professional life.

  1. _____

  2. _____

  3. _____

  4. _____

  5. _____

- How Have You Used Your Strengths in the Past?

Think of a time when you relied on one or more of your strengths to overcome a challenge. Describe the situation and how your strengths helped you succeed.

_____
_____
_____
_____

- Recognize Opportunities to Use Your Strengths:
  What is a current challenge or goal you're facing? How can you apply your strengths to tackle it?

_____
_____
_____
_____

- Celebrate Your Unique Strengths:
  Take a moment to celebrate what makes you unique. Write a positive affirmation that reminds you of the value of your strengths.

_____
_____
_____
_____

- Set a Goal:
   How can you use one of your strengths more effectively over the next month? Set a specific goal that allows you to leverage this strength in a new way.

_____

_____

_____

_____

_____

_____

Remember, confidence starts with knowing and playing to your strengths. Embrace them, amplify them, and use them to build the life you want. You already have everything you need to succeed—it's time to trust in yourself.

* * *

CHAPTER 2
PRACTICE MAKES PERMANENT

UNDERSTANDING THE STRATEGY:

We often hear the phrase "practice makes perfect," but that's not always true—perfection is elusive, and striving for it can lead to disappointment. What *is* true is that "practice makes permanent." This means that whatever you practice regularly becomes a part of you, solidified in your habits, actions, and mindset. The more you practice something, the more it becomes automatic, ingrained in how you move through the world.

When it comes to confidence, practice is essential. Confidence isn't something that magically appears—it's built over time through consistent action. Whether you're practicing a skill, developing a habit, or reinforcing a mindset, the key to lasting confidence is repetition. The more you do something, the more familiar it becomes, and the more comfortable and confident you feel.

It's easy to look at confident people and think they were born that way, but confidence is a muscle. Like any other muscle, it grows stronger the more you work it. The actions you take, the challenges you face, and even the way you talk to yourself every day are all forms of practice. If you're constantly practicing self-doubt or fear, those thoughts will become permanent. But if you practice self-belief, resilience, and courage, those qualities will become a part of who you are.

Building confidence through practice isn't just about big, life-changing moments. It's about the small, consistent actions you take daily. It's about showing up, even when you don't feel ready, and doing the work again and again until it becomes second nature. Just as athletes practice improving their performance, you can practice confidence in every area of your life.

CONSISTENCY IS KEY:

One of the most crucial elements of practice is consistency. Doing something once is not enough to foster lasting confidence. Genuine confidence stems from committing time, effort, and dedication to continuous improvement. Consistency generates momentum, and with that momentum comes a sense of progress and achievement that reinforces your confidence.

Think about the first time you tried something new—whether it was a new sport, skill, or job. You likely didn't feel very confident at first. But as you practiced and became more familiar with what you were doing, your confidence grew. It's the same with anything in life. The more you practice, the more comfortable you become, and the more confidence you build.

Consistency also means showing up even when you don't feel like it. There will be days when you doubt yourself, when you don't feel motivated, or when you question whether you're making progress. But those are the moments when practice matters most. When you push through the discomfort and keep going, you're teaching yourself that you are capable, and that's where real confidence is born.

REPETITION BREEDS MASTERY:

Confidence is often tied to competence. The more you repeat something, the better you become at it, and the more confident you feel in your ability to succeed. Whether you're practicing a skill or reinforcing a positive mindset, repetition is the key to mastery. When you've done something enough times, it becomes second nature, and you no longer have to think about it—you just do it.

Think about athletes who perform under pressure. They don't rely on luck—they rely on the thousands of hours of practice they've put in. By the time they step onto the court, field, or stage, their movements are automatic, built from muscle memory and mental conditioning. Confidence in high-pressure situations comes from knowing that you've practiced enough to handle whatever comes your way.

The same principle applies to life. If you want to feel confident in your job, in your relationships, or in pursuing your goals, you have to practice. Repetition builds confidence by turning uncertainty into familiarity and fear into action.

* * *

BOUNCE PASS TO ME:

Reflecting on my journey

Let me share a moment from my time at the University of North Carolina. It was the 1994 National Championship game, and with just seven seconds left, we were down by two points to Louisiana Tech. The pressure was immense. Were we nervous? ABSOLUTELY! Everything that we worked on for the last four years, going from the last team in the ACC to being one of the last two teams in the country still standing. All eyes were on us during the sold-out crowd and nationally televised game. But in these moments, we didn't focus on what could go wrong. We focused on our team's strength—our resilience. We had been through tight games before, and we knew we had the grit to overcome. We were all hoping for our name to be called upon to take the final shot. A time-out was called and our Head Coach, Sylvia Hatchell called a play "20's" for ME to catch a lob right in front of the rim, I was to tip the ball in for the tie to send us to overtime. We head to the court with one time-out left, with my heart pounding a hundred beats per minute. The ref handed us the ball, we executed the play and the defense switched all screens and had me covered. We quickly called another Time-Out. This time our Coach called for a play called 30s for my teammate Charlotte Smith, I was instructed to change the angle of my screen for Charlotte to shoot a three-pointer, going for the win and not the tie. "THIRTIES??", I thought to myself. I was surprised by the call because we ran it several times that game and it didn't work because they were switching all screens. I vividly remember the look on the other Coaches' faces when our Head Coach made the call to go for the win and not the tie.

Then all of a sudden, our Coach looked us all in our eyes and said, "This game is not over, we will win this game!" She put her hand out for us to join her in one final huddle. And in that moment, no matter how we felt about the call and who she chose to shoot the last shot, we all had a major part to play in winning the game, we all had to have confidence that we would win this game. I found peace in the fact that we had practiced this play a thousand times. The best part about

THE CONFIDENCE PLAYBOOK

it is that we had practiced this play against our toughest opponents... Ourselves. It's harder to practice against your teammates because they know the play, which means they also know how to defend the play. So, we had already faced anything Louisiana Tech could have possibly thrown at us to stop our play, especially switching all screens. We all put our hands in the huddle and on three we screamed: "National Champs" (just as we had all season that year). When the five players walked on the court, we did our huddle to make sure everyone was listening and understood their assignments. That's when my teammate Charlotte Smith asked me a question I will never forget. "What are we running?" she asked. "OH MY GOD, CHARLOTTE, we are running 30's for you, but instead of going to the block, I'm screening for you to shoot a three." "But they switched the last time we ran it so I'm going to screen my own man!" "Me, why me?" she asked. "I don't know but we've practiced this a thousand times, bend your knees and follow through aggressively, YOU'VE GOT THIS." We executed the final play, she hit the shot, and when the buzzer went off we were the NATIONAL CHAMPIONS!

That moment didn't just happen by chance. It happened because God was with us, and we practiced!

View the championship last second play below!

* * *

BOUNCE PASS TO YOU:
Your Turn:

This is where you get to put the principle of "practice makes permanent" into action. Take some time to reflect on areas in your life where you want to build confidence, and think about how you can start practicing consistently.

- Identify an Area for Growth:
  Think of one skill, habit, or mindset you want to develop or improve. What is it that you want to be more confident in?

_____

_____

_____

_____

- Break It Down into Small Steps:
  Confidence is built gradually, so break your goal down into manageable steps. What's the first small action you can take to start building confidence in this area?

  _____

  _____

  _____

  _____

- Commit to Consistent Practice:
  Set a schedule for yourself to practice this skill or mindset regularly. How often will you practice? Commit to practicing for at least a week, and then assess your progress.

  _____

  _____

  _____

  _____

- Track Your Progress:
  Confidence grows when you can see improvement. Keep track of how often you practice and any progress you make. At the end of each day or week, reflect on how your practice has contributed to your growing confidence.

  _____

  _____

  _____

  _____

- Stay Motivated Through Setbacks:
  There will be days when you don't feel like practicing especially when you don't see immediate results. What will you do to stay motivated and keep going during those times? Write down a plan to keep yourself on track, even when it feels difficult.

  _____
  _____
  _____
  _____

- Reflect on Past Successes:
  Think back to a time when consistent practice helped you achieve something important. What did that experience teach you about the value of practice?

  _____
  _____
  _____
  _____

- Visualize Your Progress:

Imagine how you'll feel once you've practiced enough to feel confident in this new area. How will this new skill or mindset change your life? What opportunities will it open up for you?

_____
_____
_____
_____

Remember, building confidence through practice is a lifelong journey. Whether you're learning a new skill or reinforcing a positive mindset, the more you practice, the stronger and more permanent that confidence becomes. Every step you take, no matter how small, is a step toward a more confident you.

Practice makes permanent—so start practicing today.

* * *

Your Turn:

- Think about a skill or habit you want to develop. What steps can you take to practice it consistently?

_____

_____

_____

- What are three small actions you can take each day to build confidence in this area?
1. _____
2. _____
3. _____

- How will you track your progress? Consider setting a goal to practice for the next thirty days.

_____

_____

_____

- Reflect on a time when consistent practice helped you achieve success. What did you learn from that experience?

_____

_____

_____

_____

- How do you handle setbacks in your practice? What steps can you take to stay motivated?

_____

_____

_____

_____

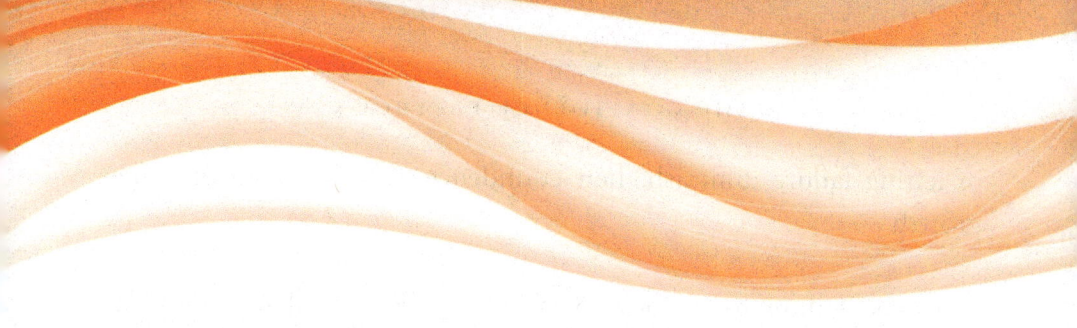

CHAPTER 3
LEARN FROM EVERY LOSS

UNDERSTANDING THE STRATEGY:

Success and confidence are not solely the result of victories. In fact, some of the most profound growth and enduring confidence emerge from the lessons gained through failure. Much like in sports, life is marked by setbacks, missed opportunities, and unexpected losses. However, it's not the losses that define us, but rather how we choose to respond to them.

The idea of "learning from every loss" is a critical strategy for building unshakeable confidence. Failure is inevitable, but instead of viewing it as the end of the road, we can choose to see it as a necessary part of our journey toward growth and success. When you learn from your losses, you turn them into valuable stepping stones that propel you forward. This mindset shift transforms failure from something to fear into something to embrace.

Many of us are conditioned to see failure as a reflection of our worth or abilities. When we fail, we might feel embarrassed, disappointed, or even question our competence. But confident people understand that setbacks are a natural part of progress. Each failure is an opportunity to learn something new, improve, and come back stronger. Instead of letting failure diminish their confidence, they use it to fuel their growth.

Consider failure as a form of feedback. Each setback offers an opportunity to ask yourself: What can I learn from this experience? How can I adjust my approach moving forward? By viewing failure as a teacher, you transform the experience from one of defeat to one of empowerment. Over time, this practice of learning from your losses will become one of your strongest sources of confidence.

RESILIENCE: THE KEY TO LEARNING FROM LOSSES

One of the most important qualities that comes from learning from failure is resilience. Resilience is the ability to bounce back after a setback and keep moving forward. It's what allows you to maintain your confidence even when things don't go your way. And just like confidence, resilience is a skill that can be developed through practice.

The more you learn to recover from losses and disappointments, the stronger your resilience becomes. This strength enables you to take risks, pursue challenging goals, and push yourself beyond your comfort zone without the fear of failure holding you back. With resilience, you develop the mindset that no matter how many times you fall, you'll always get back up stronger.

In this chapter, we'll explore how to view failure not as an end but as an essential part of the journey toward success. You'll learn how to use setbacks to your advantage and develop the resilience needed to maintain your confidence even in the face of adversity.

* * *

WHY FAILURE IS AN ESSENTIAL PART OF SUCCESS:

It's easy to look at successful people and assume that they've never failed. But the truth is, failure is often the foundation of success. Every successful person has faced setbacks, rejections, and failures along the way. What sets them apart is their ability to learn from those failures and keep going.

When you fail, it's tempting to give up or let self-doubt take over. But if you can shift your mindset and view failure as part of the process, you'll realize that each setback is bringing you closer to your goal. Failure teaches you what doesn't work, refines your approach, and makes you more resilient. It's a vital ingredient in the recipe for success.

View failure as constructive feedback. Each setback presents an opportunity to reflect: What lessons can I take from this experience? How can I refine my approach moving forward? By embracing failure as a teacher, you shift from feeling defeated to feeling empowered. Over time, this mindset of learning from setbacks becomes one of your most powerful sources of confidence.

* * *

HOW TO LEARN FROM FAILURE:

Learning from failure isn't always easy, but with the right mindset and approach, it becomes a powerful tool for growth. Here are some practical steps to help you turn losses into learning opportunities:

1. Acknowledge the Failure:
- The first step in learning from failure is to acknowledge it. Don't try to sweep it under the rug or pretend it didn't happen. Be honest with yourself about what went wrong. Admitting failure is not a sign of weakness—it's a sign of strength and maturity.

2. Reflect on the Experience:
- Take time to reflect on the situation. Ask yourself, "What could I have done differently?" "What factors contributed to this outcome?" "What can I learn from this experience?" Reflection is a crucial part of the learning process because it allows you to gain valuable insights that can inform your future actions.

3. Identify the Lesson:
- Every failure comes with a lesson. It could be something technical, like needing to improve a specific skill, or it could be something mental, like learning to manage stress or stay focused under pressure. The key is to identify the lesson and take it with you moving forward.

4. Adjust:
- Once you've identified the lesson, it's time to adjust. What changes can you implement to improve your chances of success next time? Whether it's refining your approach, changing your mindset, or seeking additional help or resources, making adjustments is a crucial step in turning failure into growth.

5. Move Forward:
- After you've reflected and adjusted, it's time to move forward. Don't dwell on the failure or let it weigh you down. Instead, use it as fuel to keep pushing toward your goals. Confidence comes from knowing that you can recover from setbacks and keep moving forward.

* * *

TURNING SETBACKS INTO CONFIDENCE:

One of the most powerful ways to cultivate confidence is by facing failure head-on and emerging stronger. Each time you recover from a setback, you prove your resilience and inner strength, reinforcing your capacity to persevere. This process creates a self-reinforcing cycle of confidence that deepens with every experience.

When you shift your mindset from fearing failure to embracing it as part of the process, you start to see every challenge as an opportunity to learn. You become less afraid to take risks, try new things, and push yourself beyond your comfort zone because you know that, even if you fail, you'll come out stronger in the end.

Over time, this practice of learning from failure builds a deep, unshakeable confidence. You'll no longer see setbacks as something to avoid or fear. Instead, you'll welcome them as opportunities to grow and improve. This is how true confidence is built—not from never failing, but from learning to thrive in the face of failure.

* * *

BOUNCE PASS TO ME
Reflecting on My Journey:

In 1991, I had the incredible honor of representing the United States at the Pan American Games, and like any athlete donning the red, white, and blue, I fully expected us to bring home the gold. After all, we were the United States—dominating women's basketball was what we were known for. But that year, things didn't go as planned. Instead of standing proudly on the top podium, watching our flag rise higher than the rest, we found ourselves in a position no U.S. women's basketball team had ever been in before: standing below the gold and silver winners, settling for a bronze medal. It was a crushing blow.

The disappointment was palpable. I'll never forget the feeling of watching the U.S. flag lowered beneath those of the other countries, knowing we had let our nation—and ourselves—down. It wasn't just that we didn't win gold; it was that we knew, deep down, we hadn't given it our all. We didn't take our opponents seriously enough. We thought we could cruise through, relying on our reputation and talent alone. The night before one of our crucial games, we were hanging out late, not fully focused on the task ahead. We assumed we'd easily handle the competition, but we were wrong.

That moment was humiliating, and it stayed with me for a long time. It wasn't just the loss—it was the lesson that came with it. I learned the hard way that no matter how skilled or prepared you think you are, you must always respect your opponents. It doesn't matter what their record is, how big or small they are, or how they've performed in the past. In that game, on that day, anyone can win if they want it more.

That loss, as painful as it was, became one of the most valuable lessons in my life. I could have let it break my confidence, but instead, I chose to use it to fuel my future successes. I promised myself I would never take another opponent lightly again, and that every time I stepped onto the court, I would be fully focused and prepared, no matter who was on the other side.

This shift in mindset was pivotal in my journey. After that experience, I went on to win multiple gold medals with Team USA in international competitions. I carried that lesson with me to every practice, every game, and every championship. I made it a point to respect every opponent, give my all in preparation, and never let complacency take root again.

Winning those gold medals meant even more to me because of the bronze I had earned in the Pan American Games. It reminded me that success is not guaranteed—it's something you earn through hard work, respect, and the ability to learn from your losses. That bronze medal wasn't the end of my story—it was the beginning of a new chapter, one where I became a more focused, driven, and resilient competitor. To this day I cherish it a little more than the others, because I have been able to inspire countless people with this story, including you.

* * *

BOUNCE PASS TO YOU
Your Turn:

Now it's your time to reflect on your own experiences with failure and how you can use those moments to build confidence. This exercise will help you shift your mindset and start viewing setbacks as opportunities for growth.

- Reflect on a Recent Failure:
  Think about a time when you experienced a setback or failure. What happened? How did it make you feel at the time?

  _____
  _____
  _____
  _____

- Identify the Lesson:
  What did you learn from that experience? Was there a specific skill, mindset, or approach that you needed to improve? Write down the lesson you took from that failure.

  _____
  _____
  _____
  _____

- Adjust:
  Based on what you learned, what changes can you make to improve your chances of success next time? How will you adjust your approach moving forward?

  _____
  _____
  _____

- Plan for Future Setbacks:

Failures and setbacks are a natural part of life. How will you handle future failures? Write down a plan for how you'll approach setbacks with resilience and a growth mindset.

_____
_____
_____
_____

- Celebrate Your Resilience:
  Think about a time when you recovered from a failure and achieved success later on. How did that experience shape your confidence? What did you learn about your own resilience?

_____
_____
_____
_____

- Shift Your Mindset:
  The next time you face a setback, how will you remind yourself that failure is a learning opportunity, not a reflection of your worth? Write down a positive affirmation that will help you stay confident, even in the face of failure.

_____
_____
_____
_____

By learning from your losses, you're not just building confidence—you're developing resilience and preparing yourself for long-term success. Remember, every setback is a setup for a comeback. Keep learning, keep growing, and keep moving forward with confidence.

* * *

CHAPTER 4
CONTROL YOUR INNER DIALOGUE

UNDERSTANDING THE STRATEGY:

One of the most powerful tools you have for building confidence is your inner dialogue—the conversations you have with yourself throughout the day. These thoughts can either lift you up and push you toward success or tear you down and keep you from reaching your potential. The way you talk to yourself in moments of stress, challenge, and uncertainty can be the deciding factor in whether you succeed or fail.

Many people aren't aware of the constant chatter in their minds. But that inner dialogue shapes how you approach everything in life—from your relationships to your career to your personal goals. When the voice in your head is filled with doubt, fear, or negativity, it's easy to lose confidence and second-guess yourself. On the other hand, when you practice positive self-talk, you build mental resilience, confidence, and the ability to face even the most difficult challenges head-on.

The key to managing your inner dialogue is developing awareness of it. Negative thoughts often slip in unnoticed, leading us to doubt ourselves, criticize our abilities, or fear the worst without realizing it. However, once you become conscious of these thoughts, you can challenge them and replace them with positive, empowering messages.

Think of your mind as a garden. If you let negative thoughts, take root, they'll grow like weeds, choking out your confidence. But if you plant seeds of positivity, self-belief, and encouragement, you'll create a mental environment where confidence can flourish. The good news is you have the power to control what you plant in your mind. You can choose to replace negative, unhelpful thoughts with ones that lift you up, strengthen your resolve, and keep you moving forward.

Learning to master your inner dialogue is a lifelong practice, but it's one of the most transformative habits you can develop. Once you get control over your thoughts, you gain control over your actions, decisions, and, ultimately, your success.

THE POWER OF POSITIVE SELF-TALK:

Positive self-talk isn't about ignoring reality or pretending that everything is perfect; it's about choosing to focus on what you can control and what actions you can take, rather than dwelling on fear, doubt, or external factors. When faced with a challenge, your inner dialogue can be your greatest ally or your worst enemy. Allowing negative thoughts to dominate can leave you feeling defeated before you even start. Conversely, practicing positive, constructive self-talk empowers you to confront challenges with confidence, giving you the best chance for success.

Here's the truth: You're going to have moments of doubt. Everyone does. But what separates confident people from those who let fear control them is how they respond to those doubts. Instead of letting negative thoughts take root, confident people challenge them and replace them with affirmations of strength, capability, and perseverance.

Bounce Pass to Me

REFLECTING ON MY JOURNEY:

One of the most vivid examples of how controlling my inner dialogue made a difference was during a game I played in Seoul, Korea for Woori Bank. At the end of the game, I learned I was just one point shy of winning the MVP of the third round. The prize? A $2,000 check. That kind of reward was more than just a bonus—it was a reflection of the hard work and dedication I'd put into my performance.

With just a few moments left in the game, I saw my coach sending a substitute to the scorer's table to take me out. My teammates, fully aware of how close I was to that MVP prize, were shouting at me to score one more basket. I knew I had to make it happen. I drove to the basket, and the referee blew the whistle, calling a foul. I was going to the line to shoot two free throws.

As I stood at the line, the ref handed me the ball, and I went through my usual free-throw routine. But to my shock, I missed the first shot. I couldn't believe it. How could I miss such a crucial free throw? Was I trying to blow this? Did I not want the extra $2,000? All of these sarcastic and negative thoughts ran through my mind in a matter of seconds, and the pressure mounted as I realized what was at stake.

Then, the substitution buzzer went off. The sub told the referee she was coming in for the shooter—*me*. Suddenly, I was sweating bullets. I had one more shot to get this right before I was taken out of the game.

But instead of letting those negative thoughts paralyze me, I knew I had to take control of my inner dialogue. So, I did something different. I stepped off the line, broke my usual routine (because as they say, insanity is doing the same thing over and over and expecting a different result), and had a full-blown conversation with myself right there on the court. I started replacing all of the sarcastic and negative thoughts with positive, empowering ones.

"You WILL hit this next shot. Bend your knees and knock it down. You can rest after this shot when your sub comes in for you. You ARE the MVP of the third round. Let's go, Ref, give me the ball so I can knock this down real quick!"

In that moment, I was fully in control of my mind, emotions, and focus. The referee bounced-passed me the ball, and with full confidence, I stepped up to the line and knocked down the second free throw. The crowd erupted, my teammates cheered, and I was subbed out with a smile on my face.

After the game, they handed me a check for $2,000, and the crowd chanted "M.V.P." It seemed to everyone else that I had hit that free throw so effortlessly, like I'd done it a thousand times before. But the truth is, the outcome of that moment came down to my inner dialogue. If I hadn't interrupted my negative thoughts and replaced them with positive, focused ones, I might have missed that shot, missed the MVP title, and missed out on the prize.

That experience taught me a powerful lesson that I've carried with me ever since: the conversations you have with yourself matter. They can either push you toward success or sabotage your efforts. What could have been a moment of failure became a moment of triumph because I mastered my inner dialogue. I call this process **#THOTWERK**— the act of transforming your thoughts to work for you, not against you.

* * *

HOW TO CONTROL YOUR INNER DIALOGUE:

Mastering your inner dialogue takes practice, but once you develop this skill, you'll find that it's one of the most effective ways to build confidence and resilience. Here's how you can start:

1. Become Aware of Your Thoughts:
- The first step in controlling your inner dialogue is awareness. Pay attention to the thoughts that come up, especially in moments of stress, challenge, or pressure. Are your thoughts lifting you up or tearing you down? Are you encouraging yourself, or are you filling your mind with doubt and negativity?

2. Challenge Negative Thoughts:
- When you notice a negative thought, challenge it. Ask yourself: "Is this thought helping me?" "Is this thought true?" Often, negative thoughts are based on fear, insecurity, or past experiences, not reality. By challenging them, you can begin to replace them with more empowering thoughts.

3. Replace Negative Thoughts with Positive Affirmations:
- Once you've identified and challenged the negative thoughts, replace them with positive affirmations. These can be simple statements like, "I am capable," "I've prepared for this," or "I can handle this." Positive affirmations help rewire your brain to focus on what's possible, rather than what's limiting.

4. Visualize Success:
- Along with positive affirmations, visualization is a powerful tool for controlling your inner dialogue. When you picture yourself succeeding, your mind starts to believe that success is not only possible but inevitable. Visualization helps you stay calm, focused, and confident in the moment.

5. Practice Gratitude:
- Gratitude is a great way to shift your mindset. When you're focused on what you're grateful for, it's harder for negative thoughts to take over. In moments of self-doubt, remind yourself of your strengths, past successes, and the things you're thankful for. Gratitude helps you stay grounded in positivity.

BOUNCE PASS TO YOU

Your Turn:

Now that you've learned the power of controlling your inner dialogue, it's time to put it into practice. Take some time to reflect on how your thoughts affect your confidence and how you can start replacing negative thoughts with positive ones.

- Become Aware of Your Inner Dialogue:
  Take a moment to reflect on your most common thoughts during stressful situations. Are they positive or negative? Write down three negative thoughts you often have in moments of pressure.

  1. _____
  2. _____
  3. _____

- Challenge and Replace Negative Thoughts:
  Now, rewrite each of those negative thoughts as a positive affirmation.

  1. _____
  2. _____
  3. _____

- Practice Positive Self-Talk:
  The next time you face a challenge, consciously replace negative thoughts with positive ones. What are three affirmations you can use to encourage yourself in tough moments?

  1. _____
  2. _____
  3. _____

- Visualize Success:
Think of an upcoming challenge or goal. Close your eyes and visualize yourself succeeding. What does it look like? How do you feel? Write down your visualization.

_____

_____

_____

_____

_____

- Reflect on Past Successes:
Think back to a time when

* * *

CHAPTER 5
VISUALIZE YOUR SUCCESS

UNDERSTANDING THE STRATEGY:

Visualization is one of the most powerful tools for building confidence and achieving success. It's more than just imagining what you want to happen—it's about mentally rehearsing the steps you need to take to reach your goal. When you visualize success, you train your mind to believe that the outcome you're aiming for is not only possible but inevitable. Your brain starts to build mental muscle memory, preparing your body to act with confidence and precision when it's time to perform.

Athletes, performers, and high achievers often use visualization to enhance their performance. By mentally rehearsing a successful outcome, they prime their minds and bodies to respond effectively under pressure. Visualization doesn't just give you a sense of calm and focus—it's also a way to build resilience, handle stress, and strengthen the belief that you are capable of achieving your goals.

The key to effective visualization is detail. It's not enough to simply imagine the result; you have to picture every step along the way. What do you see? What do you feel? What sounds are around you? The more vividly you can create the scene in your mind, the more your brain believes it's real. And when your brain believes in the possibility of success, your body follows suit.

In this chapter, you'll learn how to harness the power of visualization to build confidence and prepare for success, even in high-pressure situations. Whether it's preparing for a big presentation, a game, or a personal challenge, visualization can help you feel calm, focused, and ready to achieve your goals.

(Bounce Pass to Me)

REFLECTING ON MY JOURNEY:

One of the most defining moments of my basketball career was my blindfolded dunk in the first-ever women's Slam Dunk Contest. It wasn't just a physical feat—it was a mental triumph, and visualization played a massive role in my success that day.

I remember deciding to enter the contest with a move that no one would expect: a blindfolded dunk. Dunking was one of my strengths—my ability to jump and my creativity on the court set me apart from others. But adding the blindfold? That took it to a whole new level. I knew if I could pull it off, it would be something people would remember forever. It wasn't just about my athletic ability anymore; it was about my mental strength, focus, and preparation.

In the weeks leading up to the contest, I practiced the dunk over and over, tirelessly. There were times when my legs were burnt out from dunking too much, especially while balancing practice and games during the season. My body was exhausted, and my hands were sore from gripping the rim. I'd dunked so much that my fingers had blistered, and some days my hands were raw and bleeding. But I knew that to succeed, I had to keep pushing.

When my body couldn't handle any more physical practice, I turned to mental practice. That's where visualization came in. I'd sit quietly and go through every single detail of the dunk in my mind. I saw myself under the basket, taking ten precise steps to my spot. I visualized my sister tying the blindfold around my eyes, just tight enough that I couldn't see anything, but still loose enough to feel comfortable. I pictured the ball in my hands, the weight of it, and the feel of the leather as I dribbled it.

In my mind, I played out every second of the dunk, from the way I would take my first dribble to the exact rhythm of my steps leading up to the basket. I could feel the court beneath my feet and hear the sounds of the crowd in the background. I envisioned myself leaping into the air, trusting that my body knew where the rim was, and throwing the ball down with perfect precision.

I did this mental rehearsal a hundred times, long before I ever attempted the blindfolded dunk in front of a crowd. Every time I visualized the dunk, I saw myself succeeding. I imagined the roar of the crowd, the excitement of my teammates, and the disbelief on people's faces when they realized I had done it.

But it wasn't just about picturing the moment of success—I also visualized overcoming the challenges along the way. There were times during practice when I wasn't sure if I could pull it off. My legs felt like lead, and my arms were sore from all the attempts. I would get frustrated, thinking, "What if I miss?" or "What if I don't jump high enough?" But every time those doubts crept in, I'd use visualization to replace them with certainty. I would see myself nailing the dunk again in my mind, and I'd talk myself through it: "You've got this. You've done it before. You can do it again."

When the day of the contest finally arrived, I was as ready as I could be. As I stood on the court, blindfold in hand, I felt the pressure of the moment. I knew all eyes were on me, and the stakes were high. But instead of letting fear take over, I leaned on my visualization. I had seen myself complete the dunk a hundred times in my mind, and now it was time to bring that mental image to life.

I took the ten steps to my spot, just like I had visualized. My sister tied the blindfold, and I dribbled the ball exactly as I had practiced. As I took off toward the basket, I trusted my body to remember everything I had rehearsed. I jumped, extended my arm, and threw the ball down into the hoop. The crowd erupted in cheers, and I could feel the energy all around me.

To the audience, it might have seemed like I pulled off the blindfolded dunk effortlessly. But the truth is, I had already succeeded in my mind long before that day. Visualization had prepared me not just physically, but mentally, to handle the pressure and execute the dunk with confidence. That day I made history by winning the first ever female slam dunk contest. It wasn't just a victory in the contest—it was a victory of mind over matter.

QR Code to the Blindfold Dunk Video
https://youtu.be/Gk7dh7HEtek?si=OTggAuS9tg_fa03L

* * *

HOW TO VISUALIZE YOUR SUCCESS:

Visualization is a simple yet powerful technique that can help you build confidence, reduce stress, and prepare for success in any area of life. Here's how you can start using visualization to achieve your goals:

1. Find a Quiet Space:
- Visualization works best when you're in a quiet, calm environment where you can focus without distractions. Find a comfortable place where you can sit or lie down and relax.

2. Create a Clear Mental Picture:
- Close your eyes and imagine yourself in a situation where you want to succeed. Be as detailed as possible. What do you see? Who is there? What sounds do you hear? What sensations do you feel? Picture every aspect of the scene.

3. Focus on the Process, Not Just the Outcome:
- Don't just visualize the moment of success—visualize the steps it takes to get there. If you're preparing for a big game, imagine every play, every movement, and every decision leading up to your victory. This prepares your mind and body to handle the entire process.

4. Feel the Emotions:
- Engage your emotions during visualization. How do you feel as you're working toward your goal? How does it feel when you succeed? Visualizing the emotions of success makes the experience feel more real and reinforces your belief in your ability to achieve it.

5. Use All Your Senses:
- Visualization is most effective when you engage all of your senses. Picture the sights, but also imagine the sounds, smells, and physical sensations of the moment. The more vivid and realistic your mental image, the more powerful it becomes.

6. Practice Regularly:
- Just like any other skill, visualization gets stronger with practice. Make it a part of your routine to visualize your goals every day, even if only for a few minutes. The more you practice, the more confident you'll feel when the time comes to perform.

* * *

BOUNCE PASS TO YOU

Your Turn:
Now it's time for you to put the power of visualization into practice. Use the following prompts to guide your mental rehearsal and prepare for success in any area of your life.

- Choose a Goal or Challenge:
  Think about an upcoming goal or challenge you want to succeed in. What is it, and why is it important to you?

_____
_____
_____

- Create a Mental Picture:
  Close your eyes and visualize the moment of success. What do you see? What sounds are around you? How does your body feel? Write down the details of your visualization.

  _____
  _____
  _____
  _____

- Visualize the Process:
  What steps do you need to take to reach your goal? Visualize yourself successfully completing each step. What challenges might come up, and how will you overcome them?

  _____
  _____
  _____

- Engage Your Emotions:
  How do you feel as you work toward your goal? How do you feel when you succeed? Describe the emotions you experience during your visualization.

  _____
  _____
  _____
  _____

- Practice Daily:
Set aside time each day to visualize your success. How will you incorporate visualization into your routine? Write down your plan.

_____

_____

_____

_____

Visualization is a powerful tool that prepares both your mind and body for success. By imagining the process and the outcome in vivid detail, you give yourself the confidence to achieve your goals in real life. Keep practicing, and soon, what you've visualized will become your reality.

* Special Bonus for all you NFT Collectors
My SLAM 00 NFT Collection is a limited edition purchased with Ethereum cryptocurrency. There is only a certain amount minted, once gone they are gone forever. It is a collection of four.
Collect one and get my SLAM 00 NFT deposited in your crypto wallet.
Collect the 2nd one and get my digital trading card in your crypto wallet.
Collect the 3rd one, and get my smart T-shirt
Collect the 4th one and get thirty minutes in my Metaverse space with ME to meet me and ask any question you want.

https://slam00.vercel.app/

* * *

CHAPTER 6
SURROUND YOURSELF WITH CHAMPIONS

UNDERSTANDING THE STRATEGY:

Building confidence isn't something you do alone. The people you surround yourself with play a massive role in shaping your mindset, influencing your actions, and ultimately determining your success. Just as a basketball team needs each player to contribute to the win, you need the right people around you to help fuel your growth and support your journey.

Surrounding yourself with champions means creating a network of people who lift you, challenge you, and push you to be your best. These are individuals who believe in your potential, celebrate your victories, and hold you accountable when necessary. They see the best in you—even when you struggle to see it yourself—and they remind you of your strengths and capabilities when you're faced with doubt.

It's often said that you become the average of the five people you spend the most time with. If you're surrounded by negativity, fear, and doubt, it's easy for those feelings to creep into your mindset. But if you're surrounded by positivity, encouragement, and ambition, you'll naturally begin to adopt those traits. Champions inspire you to aim higher, think bigger, and strive for greatness.

It's important to remember that a champion is not just someone who has achieved great things themselves; it's someone who genuinely wants to see *you* succeed. Whether it's a mentor, coach, friend, or family member, champions are those who push you to reach your full potential while offering support, wisdom, and guidance along the way.

In this chapter, you'll learn how to build a network of champions and why this support system is essential for long-term success. You'll also explore the importance of becoming a champion for others and how lifting others up strengthens your own confidence.

* * *

BOUNCE PASS TO ME:

Reflecting on My Journey:

Throughout my career, I've had the privilege of being surrounded by champions. From my college days at the University of North Carolina to my professional career in the WNBA and overseas, the people I had in my corner made all the difference. Their belief in me, their encouragement, and their unwavering support were critical to my growth as an athlete and as a person.

One moment that stands out vividly is during my time playing overseas. I had the incredible opportunity to play in various countries, but it wasn't always easy. The culture shock, the language barriers, and the pressure to perform in foreign environments could have easily gotten into my head. But during my time in Seoul, Korea, I was fortunate to have a team that felt more like a family and a coach who believed in my abilities beyond what I sometimes believed in myself.

When I was preparing for the Slam Dunk Contest, the encouragement from my teammates was a game-changer. I wasn't just competing for myself—I was carrying the pride of my team, and their belief in me became my belief in myself. My sister, who helped me tie the blindfold, was my support system in more ways than one. She didn't just help me with the physical part of the dunk—she was with me mentally and emotionally, offering reassurance when I needed it most.

I'll never forget the moments of doubt I had before the contest. There were days when I felt exhausted—my body was sore, my legs heavy from practice, and my hands blistered from gripping the ball and rim over and over again. But my team always had my back. They'd encourage me to rest, recover, and come back stronger. On the days when I didn't feel like I had anything left to give, their encouragement pushed me to keep going.

Today, I have the luxury of being married to the Champion of our household. My Husband, Brian Spann. He is my MVP, I know that he gives advice and support with my very best interest in mind. Not only is he my Husband, but he is my friend and business partner as well. It is important to date and ultimately marry someone who brings support, wisdom, and accountability into your everyday life. It helps if the person you're with is your biggest cheerleader. I can honestly say I have that within my own home starting with my spouse and parents.

Having champions around me didn't just help me succeed in the contest—it helped me thrive throughout my career. From winning gold medals to coaching future champions, I've seen firsthand how the people you surround yourself with can make all the difference. Their belief in me became my belief in myself, and that's why I continue to surround myself with champions in every area of my life.

* * *

BUILDING YOUR NETWORK OF CHAMPIONS:

Building a strong support system of champions doesn't happen overnight. It takes time, effort, and intentionality. You need to surround yourself with people who truly want to see you succeed and who aren't afraid to push you toward your potential.

Here's how you can start building your network of champions:

1. Seek Out Mentors:
- Find people who have achieved success in the areas where you want to grow. These mentors can offer guidance, wisdom, and advice based on their own experiences. Look for people who inspire you and whose values align with your own.

2. Foster Positive Relationships:
- Champions are not just mentors or coaches—they can be friends, family members, or colleagues who believe in you and offer support.

Surround yourself with people who encourage you, motivate you, and genuinely want to see you succeed.

3. Be Selective with Your Inner Circle:
- Not everyone deserves a place in your inner circle. Choose people who bring positivity, energy, and encouragement to your life. Steer clear of those who bring negativity, doubt, or unnecessary criticism. Your environment matters, and the people you surround yourself with have a direct impact on your confidence.

4. Offer Support in Return:
- Building a network of champions is a two-way street. Be willing to offer support, encouragement, and accountability to others. When you lift others up, you not only strengthen their confidence—you also build your own. Becoming a champion for others creates a positive cycle of growth for everyone involved.

5. Be Open to Feedback and Growth:
- Champions don't just tell you what you want to hear—they tell you what you need to hear. Be open to constructive feedback from your mentors and supporters. Growth comes from being willing to listen, learn, and make the necessary adjustments to improve.

* * *

THE POWER OF ACCOUNTABILITY:

One of the greatest gifts champions offer is accountability. When you have people in your life who hold you accountable, you're more likely to stay focused, motivated, and consistent in your efforts. Champions don't let you settle for mediocrity—they push you to be your best, even when it's uncomfortable.

Accountability partners play a crucial role in helping you set goals, track your progress, and uphold your commitments. They celebrate your successes while also holding you accountable when you're not giving your best effort. This kind of tough love is essential for growth, highlighting the importance of surrounding yourself with champions who support and challenge you.

When you're accountable to someone else, you're more likely to stay on track and follow through on your goals. Champions keep you honest and push you to keep striving for greatness.

* * *

BECOMING A CHAMPION FOR OTHERS:
Surrounding yourself with champions is important, but equally important is becoming a champion for others. When you support and uplift the people around you, you create a culture of confidence and success. Being a champion for others isn't just about giving praise—it's about challenging them to grow, offering constructive feedback, and celebrating their achievements along the way.

When you assist others in building their confidence, you simultaneously strengthen your own. By recognizing the strengths in others and understanding how they contribute to the bigger picture, you enrich your perspective. Whether through mentoring a younger teammate, supporting a friend in need, or encouraging a colleague, championing others creates a ripple effect of positivity and success.

* * *

BOUNCE PASS TO YOU

Your Turn:
Now it's your time to reflect on the champions in your life and how you can build a strong support system. Use the following prompts to guide your thoughts and actions:

- **Identify Your Champions:**
  Who are the people in your life who encourage and support you? Write down the names of the individuals who push you to be your best.

  1. _____
  2. _____
  3. _____
  4. _____
  5. _____

- **Reflect on Their Impact:**
  How have these champions influenced your confidence and success? What specific ways have they helped you grow or achieve your goals?

  _____
  _____
  _____
  _____

- **Evaluate Your Inner Circle:**
  Are there any relationships in your life that drain your energy or undermine your confidence? How can you set boundaries to protect your mental and emotional well-being?

- **Find a Mentor:**
  If you don't have a mentor or role model, who can you reach out to for guidance and support? Write down the names of potential mentors and think about how you can begin building a relationship with them.

- **Be a Champion for Others:**
  How can you be a champion for someone else? Identify one person in your life who could use your support or encouragement. What specific actions can you take to help them build confidence and reach their goals?

- **Set Accountability Goals**:
Write down one goal you're currently working toward. Who can you ask to help hold you accountable for reaching this goal?

_____

_____

_____

_____

_____

_____

By surrounding yourself with champions and becoming a champion for others, you'll create a powerful support system that fuels your confidence and success. Remember, champions lift each other up—and when you have people who believe in you, there's nothing you can't achieve.

* * *

CHAPTER 7
CELEBRATE YOUR WINS

UNDERSTANDING THE STRATEGY:

Celebrating your wins is one of the most important steps in building and maintaining confidence. Success, no matter how big or small, deserves recognition. Whether you've achieved a major milestone or simply made it through a tough day, each victory is worth celebrating because it strengthens your belief in yourself and your ability to keep moving forward.

Many people tend to brush past their accomplishments without fully acknowledging them. They're so focused on the next goal, the next challenge, or the next step that they forget to appreciate how far they've come. But here's the truth: confidence is built not just in moments of achievement, but in the act of acknowledging and celebrating those achievements.

When you take the time to celebrate your wins, you reinforce the positive actions, decisions, and habits that led to success. You remind yourself that you are capable, that your efforts pay off, and that you are moving in the right direction. This process is crucial because it boosts your motivation, keeps you focused, and strengthens your mental resilience for future challenges.

Celebration is not just about throwing a party or rewarding yourself with something extravagant. It's about taking a moment to pause, reflect, and feel gratitude for what you've accomplished. It's about recognizing your growth and acknowledging the hard work, persistence, and determination that got you there.

In this chapter, you'll learn how to celebrate your wins in meaningful ways and why this practice is essential for long-term confidence. You'll also explore how celebrating small victories can lead to even bigger successes.

* * *

REFLECTING ON MY JOURNEY:

Throughout my career, I learned the importance of celebrating wins, both big and small. As an athlete, it's easy to get caught up in the cycle of always striving for the next goal, the next championship, the next victory. But if you don't take the time to appreciate the journey and celebrate along the way, you miss out on the joy and fulfillment that come from your achievements.

One of my most memorable moments came after I completed the blindfolded dunk in the first-ever women's Slam Dunk Contest. When I finally stepped onto the court and nailed that dunk, the feeling of triumph was indescribable. The crowd erupted, my teammates cheered, and the judges handed me the $5,000 check. After the contest, I didn't just move on to the next goal. I took the time to celebrate. I reflected on all the hard work, dedication, and sacrifices that had led to that moment. I allowed myself to fully appreciate the achievement and to soak in the pride and joy of knowing I had pushed myself beyond what I thought was possible.

CHAPTER 7
CELEBRATE YOUR WINS

UNDERSTANDING THE STRATEGY:

Celebrating your wins is one of the most important steps in building and maintaining confidence. Success, no matter how big or small, deserves recognition. Whether you've achieved a major milestone or simply made it through a tough day, each victory is worth celebrating because it strengthens your belief in yourself and your ability to keep moving forward.

Many people tend to brush past their accomplishments without fully acknowledging them. They're so focused on the next goal, the next challenge, or the next step that they forget to appreciate how far they've come. But here's the truth: confidence is built not just in moments of achievement, but in the act of acknowledging and celebrating those achievements.

When you take the time to celebrate your wins, you reinforce the positive actions, decisions, and habits that led to success. You remind yourself that you are capable, that your efforts pay off, and that you are moving in the right direction. This process is crucial because it boosts your motivation, keeps you focused, and strengthens your mental resilience for future challenges.

Celebration is not just about throwing a party or rewarding yourself with something extravagant. It's about taking a moment to pause, reflect, and feel gratitude for what you've accomplished. It's about recognizing your growth and acknowledging the hard work, persistence, and determination that got you there.

In this chapter, you'll learn how to celebrate your wins in meaningful ways and why this practice is essential for long-term confidence. You'll also explore how celebrating small victories can lead to even bigger successes.

* * *

REFLECTING ON MY JOURNEY:

Throughout my career, I learned the importance of celebrating wins, both big and small. As an athlete, it's easy to get caught up in the cycle of always striving for the next goal, the next championship, the next victory. But if you don't take the time to appreciate the journey and celebrate along the way, you miss out on the joy and fulfillment that come from your achievements.

One of my most memorable moments came after I completed the blindfolded dunk in the first-ever women's Slam Dunk Contest. When I finally stepped onto the court and nailed that dunk, the feeling of triumph was indescribable. The crowd erupted, my teammates cheered, and the judges handed me the $5,000 check. After the contest, I didn't just move on to the next goal. I took the time to celebrate. I reflected on all the hard work, dedication, and sacrifices that had led to that moment. I allowed myself to fully appreciate the achievement and to soak in the pride and joy of knowing I had pushed myself beyond what I thought was possible.

THE CONFIDENCE PLAYBOOK

That moment wasn't just about winning the contest—it was about honoring the journey that led to it. I had practiced tirelessly, fought through self-doubt, and worked on my mental toughness through visualization and positive self-talk. All of those steps, big and small, deserved celebration.

Celebrating that win didn't just boost my confidence for the next challenge—it reminded me of what I was capable of. It reinforced the belief that when I put in the work, stay focused, and trust in my abilities, I can achieve great things. That mindset carried me through many other challenges in my career, both on and off the court.

But it's not just the big wins that matter. I've learned that small victories are just as important. There were times during my career when I struggled with injuries or faced setbacks that made me question my path. In those moments, I learned to celebrate the little things: a good practice session, winning an overtime game, or simply showing up on a tough day. Those small wins kept me going and reminded me that every step forward counts.

* * *

WHY CELEBRATING YOUR WINS MATTERS:

Celebrating your wins is about more than just feeling good at the moment—it's about building a foundation of confidence that will carry you through future challenges. Here are a few reasons why celebrating your wins is so important:

1. **Reinforces Positive Habits and Behaviors:**
- When you take the time to celebrate your achievements, you reinforce the habits, actions, and decisions that led to success. This helps you build a strong foundation for future growth and success. By recognizing what worked, you're more likely to continue those positive behaviors.

2. **Boosts Motivation:**
- Celebrating your wins gives you a sense of accomplishment and fuels your motivation to keep going. It's easy to lose steam when you're constantly pushing forward without stopping to acknowledge your progress. Celebrations provide that boost of energy you need to stay focused and committed to your goals.

3. **Builds Resilience:**
- Life is full of ups and downs, and setbacks are inevitable. But when you celebrate your wins, you strengthen your resilience. Each victory, no matter how small, serves as a reminder that you are capable of overcoming challenges and achieving success.

4. **Prevents Burnout:**
- Constantly striving for the next goal without pausing to celebrate can lead to burnout. When you take the time to acknowledge your efforts and successes, you give yourself the mental and emotional space to recharge. This balance is essential for maintaining long-term motivation and confidence.

5. **Encourages Gratitude:**
- Celebration is a form of gratitude. It's an opportunity to reflect on how far you've come and to appreciate the journey. Gratitude fosters a positive mindset and helps you stay grounded, even when the road ahead seems challenging.

* * *

CELEBRATING THE SMALL WINS:

Many people think a celebration is only for the big milestones, like winning a championship, getting a promotion, or achieving a major goal. But the truth is, small wins are just as important—if not more so—because they happen more frequently and keep you moving forward. When you celebrate small victories, you build momentum and stay motivated for the long haul.

Small wins could be anything from completing a workout when you didn't feel like it, finishing a project ahead of schedule, or learning something new that brings you closer to your goal. These moments of progress deserve recognition because they represent your commitment, effort, and perseverance.

HERE'S HOW YOU CAN START CELEBRATING THE SMALL WINS IN YOUR LIFE:

1. **Acknowledge Your Progress:**
- Take time at the end of each day or week to reflect on the progress you've made. What steps have you taken toward your goals? What challenges did you overcome? Even the smallest accomplishments deserve recognition.

2. **Reward Yourself:**
   - Celebration doesn't have to be extravagant. It could be something as simple as taking a break, treating yourself to something you enjoy, or spending time doing something that makes you happy. The key is to reward yourself in a way that feels meaningful and helps you appreciate your efforts.

3. **Share Your Wins with Others:**
   - Don't be afraid to share your victories with the people who support you. Whether it's friends, family, or colleagues, celebrating together amplifies the joy and reinforces your achievements. Plus, it's a great way to strengthen your relationships with the people who believe in you.

4. **Keep a Victory Log:**
   - Consider keeping a journal or log where you write down your wins—both big and small. This practice helps you track your progress and gives you a sense of accomplishment over time. When you're feeling discouraged or stuck, you can look back at your victory log and remind yourself of how far you've come.

* * *

BOUNCE PASS TO YOU

Your Turn:

Now it's time for you to start celebrating your own wins. Use the following prompts to reflect on your achievements and create a habit of recognizing your progress.

- **Reflect on Recent Wins:**

    What have you accomplished recently? It could be something big or small, but take a moment to acknowledge your progress. Write down three recent wins, no matter how small they may seem.

    1. _____
    2. _____
    3. _____

- **How Did You Celebrate?**

    Did you take time to celebrate these wins? If not, how can you celebrate now? What meaningful reward or acknowledgment can you give yourself?

    _____
    _____
    _____
    _____

- **Celebrate the Small Stuff:**

    Think about the small victories in your day-to-day life. What are some examples of small wins you've had recently that contributed to your overall progress? Write down a few small wins that may have gone uncelebrated.

    _____
    _____
    _____
    _____

- **Plan a Celebration:**
Choose one goal you're currently working toward. How will you celebrate when you achieve it? Write down a plan for how you'll reward yourself when you reach this milestone.

_____
_____
_____
_____
_____
_____
_____

- **Share Your Wins:**
Who can you share your victories with? Write down the names of people who support you and who would be excited to celebrate with you. How can you include them in your celebrations?

_____
_____
_____
_____
_____
_____
_____

- **Start a Victory Log:**
  Create a space where you can regularly write down your wins. How often will you update it? What will you include? Consider using a journal or app to track your progress and celebrate your victories over time.

  _____
  _____
  _____
  _____
  _____
  _____
  _____
  _____

Celebrating your wins isn't just about feeling good in the moment—it's about building long-lasting confidence and reinforcing the habits that lead to success. Whether it's a big milestone or a small step forward, every win deserves to be celebrated. So, take the time to acknowledge your achievements, reward yourself for your efforts, and keep moving forward with confidence.

CONCLUSION
THE JOURNEY TO LIFELONG CONFIDENCE

Confidence is not a destination—it's a journey, one that you actively create every single day. As we've explored throughout *The Confidence Playbook*, confidence is built through intentional strategies, thoughtful self-reflection, and the daily practice of positive habits. It's something you strengthen each time you choose to step outside of your comfort zone, face your fears, and take action, even when the path is uncertain.

The process of building confidence doesn't happen overnight, and it's not a one-size-fits-all approach. Throughout this book, you've learned that confidence comes from playing to your strengths, consistently practicing the skills you want to master, learning from your losses, controlling your inner dialogue, visualizing your success, surrounding yourself with champions, and celebrating your wins. These strategies work together to create a solid foundation for a confident, resilient, and successful life.

As you move forward, it's important to remember that confidence is fluid. There will be times when you feel on top of the world—completely sure of yourself and your abilities. And there will be moments when you face doubt, fear, or setbacks that shake your confidence. That's normal. The key is to recognize that confidence is something you can continually develop and nurture, no matter what challenges come your way.

THE POWER OF DAILY ACTION:
One of the most important lessons from *The Confidence Playbook* is that confidence is built through daily actions. It's not enough to think about what you want or hope that one day you'll feel more confident. You have to take small, consistent steps every day to reinforce your belief in yourself.

Every time you push yourself to practice a new skill, take on a challenge, or replace a negative thought with a positive one, you're strengthening your confidence muscle. Confidence grows from the accumulation of small wins, the lessons learned from failure, and the belief that, no matter what happens, you can keep moving forward.

EMBRACING SETBACKS AS PART OF THE JOURNEY:
Throughout your journey, you'll face obstacles, setbacks, and failures. But as you've learned in these pages, failure isn't something to fear—it's something to embrace. Each setback is an opportunity to learn, grow, and become more resilient. The most confident people aren't those who never fail; they're the ones who know how to bounce back, adapt, and keep going when things don't go as planned.

By embracing failure as part of the process, you remove its power to diminish your confidence. Instead, you see it as a stepping stone to success, a valuable teacher that shows you what you need to do differently next time. Confidence is not about perfection—it's about resilience, adaptability, and the ability to keep striving for greatness even when the road gets tough.

THE IMPORTANCE OF SELF-REFLECTION:

Self-reflection is a key component of building lifelong confidence. As you progress on your journey, it's essential to take time to reflect on where you've been, what you've achieved, and how you've grown. Reflect on the wins you've celebrated, the lessons you've learned from setbacks, and the people who have supported you along the way.

Self-reflection allows you to track your progress, appreciate how far you've come, and adjust your approach when needed. It's also an opportunity to reconnect with your "why"—the deeper reason behind the goals you're working toward and the vision you have for your life. By regularly reflecting on your journey, you stay aligned with your purpose and continue to grow in confidence.

LIVING WITH CONFIDENCE EVERY DAY:

Confidence is a practice. It's not something you achieve once and then have forever—it's something you choose to live with every day. Whether it's in your career, your relationships, your personal goals, or your daily mindset, confidence is a decision you make moment by moment.

Living with confidence means taking risks, stepping outside of your comfort zone, and believing in your abilities, even when the outcome is uncertain. It means trusting yourself enough to know that you can handle whatever comes your way and that you have the strength to adapt, learn, and grow no matter what challenges you face.

As you continue on your journey, remember that confidence is not about having all the answers or never feeling fear. It's about having the courage to act despite fear, to pursue your goals with passion, and to believe in your potential even when the path ahead is unclear.

* * *

PUTTING YOUR PLAYBOOK INTO ACTION:

Now that you've completed *The Confidence Playbook*, it's time to put what you've learned into action. This journey isn't about reaching a final destination—it's about continuously growing, learning, and strengthening your confidence with every step you take. Here are a few final reminders as you move forward:

1. **Play to Your Strengths:**

    Always remember what makes you unique and capable. Focus on your strengths and use them as the foundation for your confidence. The more you rely on your natural abilities, the more confident you will feel in every aspect of your life.

2. **Practice Makes Permanent:**

    Confidence is built through consistent action. Whatever you practice regularly becomes permanent, so make sure you're practicing the habits and mindsets that will strengthen your confidence.

3. **Learn from Every Loss:**

    Setbacks are part of the process. Embrace them, learn from them, and use them to grow. Every loss teaches you something valuable, and each lesson moves you closer to success.

4. **Control Your Inner Dialogue:**

    The conversations you have with yourself are powerful. Make sure your inner dialogue is one of positivity, encouragement, and belief in your abilities. Replace negative thoughts with empowering ones and watch your confidence soar.

5. **Visualize Your Success:**

    Take time to mentally rehearse your goals. Visualization helps you prepare for success and builds your belief in your ability to achieve your dreams. When you can see it in your mind, you're one step closer to making it a reality.

6. **Surround Yourself with Champions:**
Keep building and nurturing your network of champions. The people you surround yourself with have a profound impact on your confidence, so make sure you're surrounded by those who believe in you and push you to grow.

7. **Celebrate Your Wins:**
Don't forget to celebrate every victory, big or small. Acknowledging your achievements fuels your motivation and reminds you of what you're capable of. Confidence grows with each win you celebrate.

* * *

FINAL THOUGHTS:

Confidence is a journey that never truly ends—it's something you carry with you and cultivate every day. By following the strategies in *The Confidence Playbook*, you've set yourself up for success not just today, but for the rest of your life.

There will be challenges along your journey, but each one presents an opportunity for growth. As you progress, remember that confidence isn't about perfection; it's about showing up, giving your best effort, and trusting yourself at every step.

You have everything you need to be confident, resilient, and successful. The playbook is in your hands, and the next chapter of your journey is yours to write.

Now go out there and live with confidence!

ABOUT THE AUTHOR

Sylvia Crawley Spann is a former professional basketball player, coach, and mentor with a career spanning both national and international stages. As a standout player for the University of North Carolina, she led her team to a National Championship in 1994. Her success on the court continued as she went on to play professionally in the WNBA, as well as internationally in 16 different countries which include Korea, Spain, and Italy.

Sylvia is perhaps most famously known for her blindfolded dunk during the first-ever women's Slam Dunk Contest, a moment that captured the imagination of basketball fans and cemented her legacy as one of the game's most creative and fearless competitors. She also represented the United States as a member of the women's national basketball team, earning multiple gold medals and a bronze medal in the, Jones Cup, Select Team, Pan American Games and World University Games. Sylvia was named USA Basketball Player of the Year in 1997, shortly after she was named to the USA National Team where she became an Alternate for the 1998 Olympic Games.

After her playing career, Sylvia transitioned into coaching, where she has impacted countless athletes as both a head coach and an assistant coach at various collegiate programs, including Ohio State University and Boston College. Her leadership and passion for the game have not only helped her teams succeed but also inspired athletes to pursue excellence on and off the court.

Today, Sylvia Crawley Spann is dedicated to empowering others through mentorship, leadership, and advocacy. She uses her platform to foster confidence and resilience in athletes, teams, and corporations around the world, helping individuals tap into their full potential and achieve greatness.

To book Sylvia as a speaker visit www.sylviacrawley.com

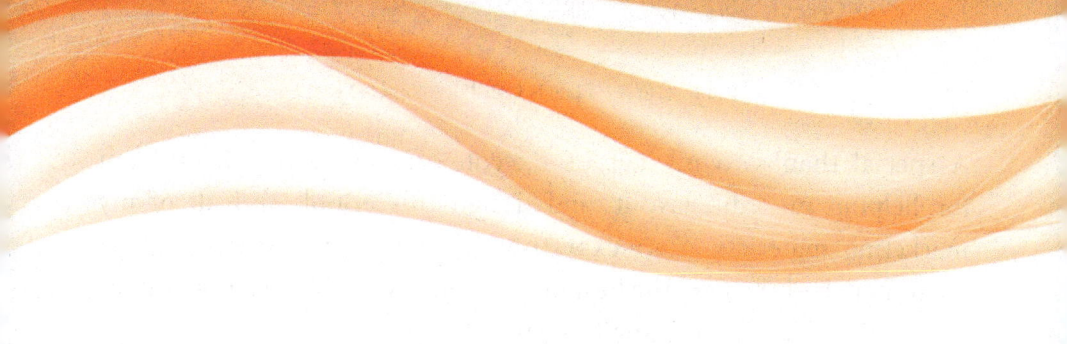

ACKNOWLEDGEMENT

First and foremost, I want to thank God, who is the head of my life and the source of all my strength, wisdom, and inspiration. Without His guidance, none of this would be possible. Every step of this journey has reflected His grace and blessings.

To my incredible husband, Brian, thank you for believing in me and supporting me throughout this entire project. Your love, encouragement, and unwavering faith in my vision have been a constant source of motivation, and I'm so grateful to have you by my side.

To my amazing parents, James and Marie, you've always been my #1 cheerleaders. From the basketball court to every endeavor I've pursued, your support and love have given me the confidence to chase my dreams. I live each day to make you both proud, and I'm forever grateful for the foundation you've provided me.

This book is dedicated to my sister, Helen, my role model, my rock, and my biggest supporter. You have been there for me mentally, financially, and spiritually from day one. Your strength, love, and guidance have carried me through the toughest times, and I couldn't have asked for a better sister and friend. #AckAck

A special thanks to my Let Us Execute and my entire Tech Team for helping me edit, layout, and design this eBook and all of my marketing materials. Your expertise, creativity, and professionalism are unmatched. You are the best in the industry, and I'm so grateful for your partnership in bringing this project to life.

Lastly, I carry the torch of my late brother, Dr. Rex L. Crawley, a humanitarian who dedicated his life to research and developing leaders. Your passion for helping others and your commitment to creating a better world continue to inspire me every day. Your legacy lives on through this work and everything I strive to achieve.

Thank you all for being a part of this journey. Your love, support, and belief in me have made this book possible.

Sylvia Crawley Spann

GLOBAL SPORTS COACH | EXPERT SPEAKER
WNBA VET

Let's Work Together

(919) 907-3518

scrawleyspann1@gmail.com

BOOK ME

Sylvia is a fun, energetic international speaker with a powerful presence. With over 23 years of experience of basketball as a National Champion, Multiple Gold Medalist, Head Basketball Coach, and ESPN2 Analyst, she uses her diversity, and skills mastered to ENERGIZE, EMPOWER, & CHALLENGE Student Bodies, Athletic Departments, and Corporations to be their very best.

Speaking Topics
Virtual/In Person

★ Confidence   ★ Leadership   ★ Recruiting   ★ Bullying
★ Mindset   ★ Accountability ★ Self Care   ★ Culture

Clients

SHAPE America

Testimonials

" SLAM signature program is a must-have and a cheat code for coaches!! Sylvia's expertise as a coach, professional athlete, and college national championship covers all aspects of helping a coach grow a program. "

" Sylvia was our guest chaplain at the Dallas Wings vs. Connecticut Sun game. To say she was good is an understatement. Her message was thought-provoking and challenging. I could see that she was penetrating the hearts of the players. "

Made in the USA
Columbia, SC
24 February 2025